Chicago Coloring

For Adults

Travel and Color

O. Jentor

First Edition - March 2017

Welcome to Chicago!

The windy city of the USA. That's Chicago.

The images are a mixture of complex and straightforward coloring outlines that most adults will find interesting.

Photos feature landmarks including the Magnificent Mile, the Marina Towers, London House, the Riverwalk, the Loop, the Pepper Canister, Michigan Avenue Bridge, Chicago Board of Trade Building, Aqua Tower and Clark Street.

Thank you for purchasing this book and I wish you many happy hours of artistic endeavour.

O Jentor

Test Page (check your materials with the paper)

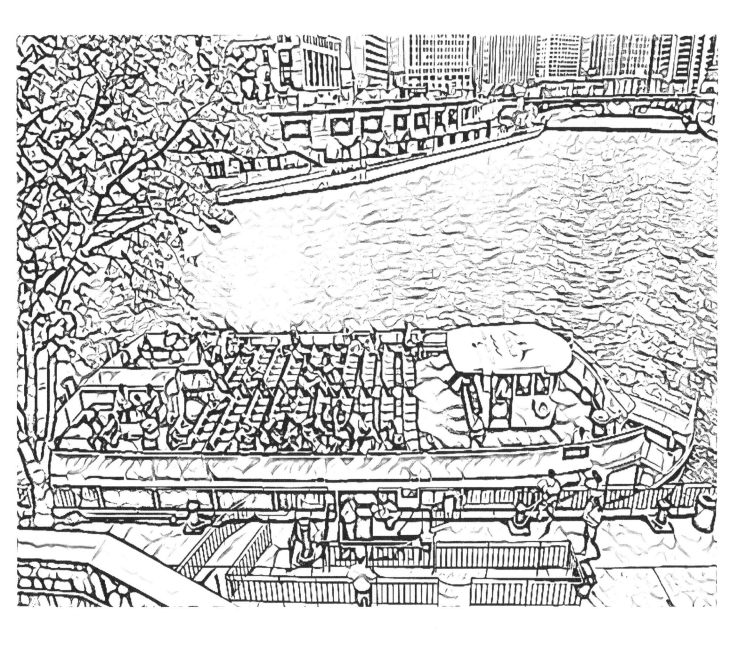

Thank you!

I hope that you enjoyed the wonderful scenes of Dublin Please check out more books by the author O Jentor featuring New York, London, San Francisco, Oxford, Barcelona, Dublin, Amsterdam, Copenhagen, Prague and Paris.

Review

Please consider to leave an honest review of this book where you purchased it. Feedback is always appreciated.

Notice of Rights

Trademarks